# JUST A FEW THINGS I LOVE ABOUT YOU (OKAY, A LOT)



LARKINROAD

Hey you,

These are just some of the countless reasons why

# I LOVE YOU

Thank you for being you, for choosing us, and for filling my life with so much joy and love.

Forever Yours

out of all the fish in the sea,

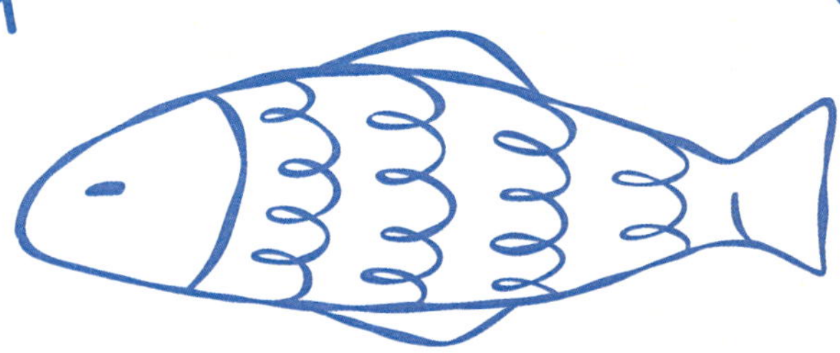

I choose you and you choose me

To: ____________________

Love: ____________________

the moment I knew you were

# special

# Something I never thank you enough for

# THREE THINGS I
# *admire*
# ABOUT YOU

1.

2.

3.

# I'M PROUD

## OF YOU FOR...

# ONE THING YOU DO THAT MAKES ME FEEL

# *Loved*

# ONE memory of us THAT ALWAYS MAKES me SMILE

# ONE THING ABOUT OUR FUTURE

THAT I'M EXCITED FOR

# One small habit of yours that I adore

# SOMETHING I'VE NEVER TOLD YOU

(BUT WANT TO...)

# My FAVORITE

memory from when we fell in love

# BEST COMPLIMENT YOU'VE EVER GIVEN ME

# One thing

I would love to do together

(that we've never done before...)

# my favorite INSIDE JOKE we share

# HOW YOU'VE CHANGED MY LIFE FOR THE BETTER

*Something*

I HOPE WE
NEVER STOP DOING

YOU MAKE ME

# LAUGH

WHEN...

# something
# I've learned about love
## because of you

YOU MAKE HARD DAYS

EASIER

WHEN YOU...

one way you make me feel

# SEEN

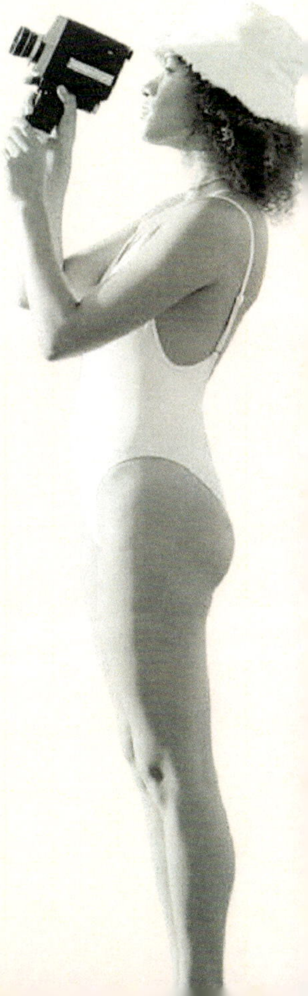

*you probably don't even realize it, but*

# I LOVE WHEN YOU